TIME FOR KIDS

African Grasslands

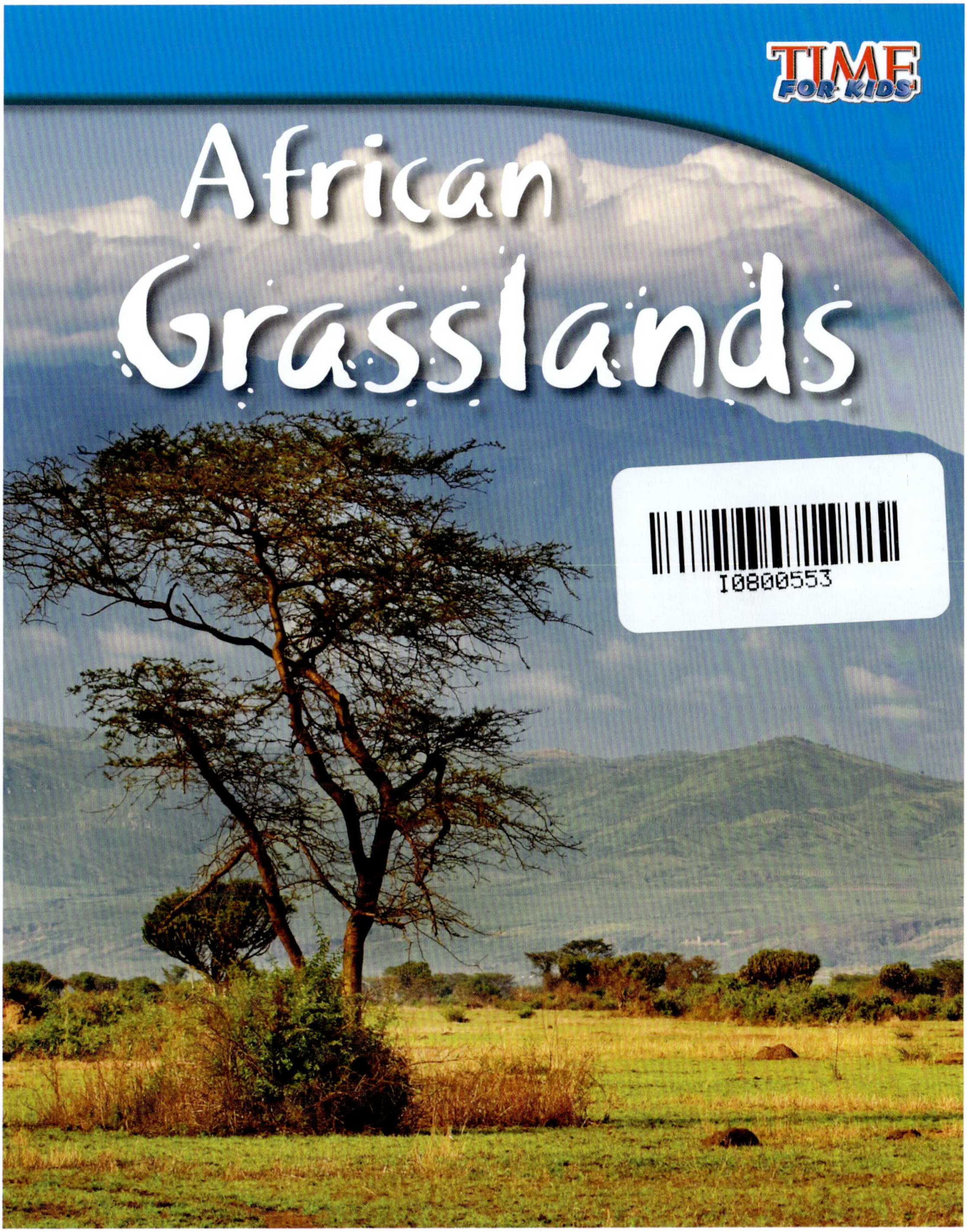

William B. Rice

Consultants

Timothy Rasinski, Ph.D.
Kent State University

Hope A. Smythe,
Environmental Scientist

Publishing Credits

Dona Herweck Rice, *Editor-in-Chief*
Robin Erickson, *Production Director*
Lee Aucoin, *Creative Director*
Conni Medina, M.A.Ed., *Editorial Director*
Jamey Acosta, *Editor*
Heidi Kellenberger, *Editor*
Lexa Hoang, *Designer*
Stephanie Reid, *Photo Editor*
Rachelle Cracchiolo, M.S.Ed., *Publisher*

Image Credits

Cover Pichugin Dmitry/Shutterstock; p.2-3 Steffen Foerster Photography/Shutterstock; p.3 gnomeandi/Shutterstock; p.4 palko72/Shutterstock; p.4-5 Oleg Znamenskiy/Shutterstock; p.5 left to right: Gerrit_de_Vries/Shutterstock; Villiers Steyn/Shutterstock; p.6-7 dp Photography/ Shutterstock; p.7 top to bottom: Sailorr/Shutterstock; palko72/Shutterstock; p.7 inset: Eky Studio/Shutterstock; p.8 Eric Gevaert/Shutterstock; p.9 Eric Isselée/Shutterstock; p.8-9 Oleg Znamenskiy/Shutterstock; p.10-11 Mitsuaki Iwago/Getty Images; p.10 Stuart Hepburn/ Shutterstock; p.11 top to bottom: NREY/Shutterstock; Winfried Winiewski/Getty Images; p.12-13 Ecoimages/Shutterstock; p.12 Alta Oosthuizen/Shutterstock; p.13 top to bottom: Hedrus/Shutterstock; Sean Nel/Shutterstock; p.14-15 Jessica Bethke/Shutterstock; p.15 top to bottom: BlueOrange Studio/Shutterstock; Sebastien Burel/Shutterstock; p.16-17 Sue Robinson/ Shutterstock; p.16 Muriel Lasure/Shutterstock; p.17 Photolibrary; p.18 left to right: EcoPrint/ Shutterstock, Photolibrary; p.18-19 Sergio Castelli/Shutterstock; p.19 top to bottom: Dinesh Valke/ Flickr; Peripitus/Wikimedia; Sylvie Lebchek/Shutterstock; Photolibrary; Alexander Bark/ Shutterstock; p.20 left to right: Uryadnikov Sergey/Shutterstock; isitsharp/iStockphoto; p.20-21 Francois van Heerden/Shutterstock; p.21 javarman/Shutterstock; p.22-23 Oleg Znamenskiy/ Shutterstock; p.22 Four Oaks/Shutterstock; p.23 Richard Peterson/Shutterstock; p.24-25 Graeme Shannon/Shutterstock; p.24 left to right: Kletr/shutterstock; xtrekx/Shutterstock; p.25 left to right: Sebastien Burel/Shutterstock; Suzi Eszterhas/ Minden Pictures; p.26-27 tigerbarb/ Shutterstock; p.26 top to bottom: Eric Isselée/Shutterstock; Cobus Olivier/Shutterstock; p.27 right: Keith Wheatley/Shutterstock; left: Pan Xunbin/Shutterstock p.28 Anna Omelchenko/ Shutterstock; p.28-29 Pichugin Dmitry/Shutterstock; p.29 lexan/Shutterstock; p.30-31 Graeme Shannon/Shutterstock; p.32 tigerbarb/Shutterstock; back cover: Richard Peterson/Shutterstock

Based on writing from *TIME For Kids.*

Teacher Created Materials
5301 Oceanus Drive
Huntington Beach, CA 92649-1030
http://www.tcmpub.com

ISBN 978-1-4333-3670-6

Printed by: VIN#973
Printed In: China PO11140

Table of Contents

Inside the Grasslands

Tall, thin grasses rustle and sway in the breeze. A herd of gazelles runs through the stalks in graceful bounds. Beside a sparkling pool of water, a long, lean lioness drinks with her cubs. In the distance, an elephant's trumpet sounds.

This is the world of the grasslands.

There are several different places where grasslands exist in Africa. One of the most beautiful and famous places is the Serengeti (ser-uhn-GET-ee) Plains. It is found in Tanzania (tan-zuh-NEE-uh), a country in eastern Africa.

What Does It Mean?

The name *Serengeti* comes from the **Maasai** (mah-SAHY) language. It means "the place where land runs on forever."

Geography and Climate

The Serengeti is usually warm and dry. However, it does rain from March to May and a little during October and November.

You are probably used to the coldest temperatures of the year being during September through March, but in the Serengeti, it is coldest between June and October.

Average Temperature

The average temperature in the Serengeti is between 55°F and 82°F.

Reversed Seasons

Earth is divided in the middle by an invisible line called the *equator*. North of the equator is the Northern Hemisphere, and south is the Southern Hemisphere. The seasons in the two hemispheres are opposites of each other. The African grasslands are in the Southern Hemisphere, so when it is summer there, it is winter in the Northern Hemisphere.

The Serengeti Plains get more than 20 inches of rain each year.

Savannas

African grasslands are also called *savannas*.

Fire and Water

The most important feature of grasslands is that they are covered by grass all year long. Grasslands also have trees and bushes, but they are scattered and spread apart. Usually, the grassland of an area has mainly one kind of tree growing on it. The types of trees can include palm, pine, and acacia (uh-KAY-shuh). The Serengeti Plains have mainly acacia trees.

How Do Animals Survive a Fire?

Most animals have a strong sense of smell and are aware of what other animals are doing. They know when there is danger, and they run. So, most animals flee before a fire reaches them. Legend has it that a rhino may even stomp out a fire before it gets too large!

Fire plays an important role on the Serengeti. Grass fires happen regularly. The parts of the grass above ground burn. But, their roots, called **rhizomes** (RAHY-zohmz), are protected by the soil and don't burn, so new grass can grow.

While the grass roots remain, other plants and trees are burned by the fires. That is one reason there is so much more grass in the grasslands than other kinds of plants.

Grass in the Serengeti can grow as tall as a grown man.

Fires on the Serengeti are common and important to the area.

The grasses, bushes, and trees are important for animals. Many of them eat these plants for food. They need them to survive.

Water is also important for all living things. Because of the wet and dry seasons and baking from the sun, the soil in some areas of the grasslands becomes as hard as rock. This hard ground is called **hardpan**. When it rains there, the water does not soak into the ground. Instead, it may pool up for many months. This provides water for the animals.

Animals such as elephants like to splash in the water and roll in the mud.

Why Do They Do That?

Why do you think animals roll and splash in the water? They do it for the same reasons you might jump in a pool, a lake, or the ocean. It keeps them cool, and they have fun, too!

A giraffe's long neck helps it reach leaves high in the trees

Ngorongoro Conservation Area

In Tanzania, there is a large area of protected grasslands. It is called the Ngorongoro (n-GOH-ron-GOH-roh) **Conservation** Area.

This area is home to the famous Ngorongoro **crater**. The crater was caused by a **volcano**. Within the crater, you can find a small grassland all its own. There are 25,000 large animals there and at least 500 types of birds.

This conservation area is known around the world for its beauty and breathtaking scenery. People travel there from all around to birdwatch, take photographs, and go on a **safari**.

Now That's Big!

The Ngorongoro crater is 2,000 feet deep! The Empire State Building could fit into the crater and still not reach its top. Even more amazing, the crater is more than 12 miles wide!

black crowned cranes

These zebras are feeding at the base of the crater.

Grassland Plants

The plains of the Serengeti and other grasslands are dotted with acacia trees. Acacias are able to survive with little water and extreme temperatures. They grow quite tall, about as high as a six-story building.

Acacias have thorny branches and white, puffy flowers. The thorns protect the flowers, leaves, and seed pods from most animals.

An acacia's deep roots go far below the ground to reach water during dry spells. Other roots just below the surface spread out wide to reach a broader area when it rains.

baobab tree

Baobab Tree

The baobab (BEY-oh-bab) is one of the biggest trees in the world. It is wider than a house and up to eight stories tall. It is tough and can survive in dry weather. It can also survive fires!

Tricky Giraffes

Giraffes are the only animals able to eat the leaves off acacia trees.

Toothbrush Tree

Toothbrush trees are another important tree of the grasslands. They have long shoots. Local people cut off the shoots when they are green. They chew on the ends until they look like toothbrushes, and then they brush their teeth with them.

Of course, grass is also very important to the grasslands. There are several types of grass growing there. The Serengeti grasses are called **sward** (swawrd), and they are especially tasty for **grazing** animals. Grasses grow well there because the roots attach strongly to the soil.

Grasses grow in both small patches and wide areas.

African feathergrass

Kinds of Grasses

There are many types of grasses in the grasslands. Here are some important ones and what makes them unique.

Name	Important Characteristics	Example
finger millet	bright green; grows nearly two feet tall	
red	dark reddish color; common on the Serengeti	
rabbit-tail fountain	blooms look like fluffy purple caterpillars	
red dropseed	seeds are layered in a pretty drop pattern	

Grassland Animals

Who are the rulers of the grasslands? The lions are, of course. Although they are called the kings of beasts, it is the females who do the hunting for the group. The males, however, are the main protectors of the **prides**.

Lions are the most **social** and cooperative of all cats. This may be one reason why they survive so well. They work and play together. But most of their time is spent sleeping.

Spotted hyenas are also social **predators**, just as lions are. The females are the leaders and protectors of the group. The largest or oldest female is the group's leader. Hyenas may be best known for their cackling laughs.

Killer Enemies

Lions and hyenas are deadly enemies. Male lions go out of their way to kill hyena clan leaders. Hyenas are major predators of lion cubs.

Vultures

Vultures are large birds that play an important part in the food web of the grasslands. They are scavengers whose main job is eating and removing rotting **carcasses**. The Lappet-faced vulture is one of the largest with a wingspan of up to ten feet.

African elephants are the big eaters of the grasslands. They eat up to 1,000 pounds of plants a day! They'll eat just about anything that's green.

Each elephant herd is made up of about 8 to 15 relatives. One female is the herd's leader. The males, however, grow much bigger than the females do.

Elephants are known for their trunks, which they use like hands. They are also known for their loud call that sounds like a trumpet.

Dung Beetles

Dung beetles help the grasslands by spreading **fertilizer** and loosening the soil for plants to grow. They find animal waste, called *dung*, that other animals leave behind. They roll it into a ball, lay an egg in it, and then bury the ball in the ground. Their new babies use some of the dung for food.

Feelings and Memories

People say that elephants never forget. This may be true. We know they have long memories. They also have feelings. Elephants cry, play, and laugh. They greet each other when they've been separated for a while. They grieve the loss of family members and other elephants.

African elephants have large, fan-like ears, thick, wrinkled skin, and long tusks made of ivory.

Giraffes are the tallest animals in the grasslands. They are best known for their long necks that help them reach food other animals cannot. They eat the leaves of acacia and other trees. Their tongues are about as long as your arm! They use them to strip the leaves from branches.

Giraffes have excellent hearing and sight, as well as a keen sense of smell. They are graceful and fast runners.

Meerkats

In the grasslands, you might see little, catlike animals perched on small hills. They are meerkats. Meerkats are cute, friendly, and helpful to one another. While other meerkats in the group look for food or sleep, one stands guard. Meerkats love to eat bugs of all kinds.

Cheetahs are built for speed. When chasing **prey** in the grasslands, they run about as fast as cars on a highway. Their paws and claws help them grip the ground. Their long, heavy tails keep them balanced when they run.

Cheetahs are probably the fastest animals on land. Their main prey are impalas and gazelles.

A cheetah trips its prey on the run and catches it as it stumbles.

Thomson's Gazelle

Thomson's gazelles have a dark side stripe and a white patch on their backsides. They are brownish on top and white on their bellies. Their coloring helps them to blend into the grasses. That is their main defense against cheetahs and other predators.

Each year, more than 1 million wildebeests (WIL-duh-beests) get together for one of the most spectacular **migrations** in the world. They migrate from the Serengeti to the open woodlands, following the rains. After all, where there is rain, there is growing grass, and wildebeests love grass!

The deep grunt of a wildebeest bull sounds like a giant croaking frog.

Rhinos and Tick Birds

Ticks and other insects are a big problem for black rhinoceroses. They dig into the rhinos' skin. So, it's a good thing that tick birds need bugs to eat. The tick birds eat the ticks and insects that climb on the rhinos. Lucky rhinos!

Termites are an important part of the Serengeti system. Termite mounds stand tall over the plains. Each mound can house over 10,000 termites. The homes are built using mud from underground. They are stuck together with termite **saliva**. Termites dig underground tunnels to get to their food. By digging underground and moving mud and soil around, termites help to make the soil healthy.

Whispering Ants

Whispering ants eat termites. When they find a termite mound, they surround it, go into the mound, and capture as many termites as possible. Whispering ants get their name from the whispering sound they make when they get upset.

Many animals use termite mounds for a good view of the surrounding area.

termites

People in the Grasslands

For centuries, no people lived in the Serengeti. About 150 years ago, the Maasai moved there from the north. They were farmers and gatherers who only hunted what they needed to live.

In the 1910s, European explorers arrived in the grasslands. Soon, European hunters came to hunt the big animals. Hunting became so popular that some animals became in danger of **extinction**. People passed laws to make the grasslands safe for animals. Now the numbers of many **endangered** animals are growing again.

Today, the people of Tanzania are working hard to protect the area. They want future generations to enjoy the wonders and beauty of the African grasslands.

The Maasai are best known for the beautiful beadwork they do and the elaborate ways they decorate their bodies.

Olduvai Gorge

The Olduvai (OHL-duh-vih) Gorge is a small canyon in the eastern Serengeti Plains. It is also an archaeological site. Louis and Mary Leakey and their son Richard are famous **archaeologists** who studied **fossils** found there. They also found and studied some of the oldest stone tools made and used by people.

Glossary

archaeologists—scientists who study old civilizations and artifacts

carcass—the dead body of an animal

conservation—activities meant to help save and protect nature and the animals living there

crater—an indentation in the earth or a mountain that is caused by volcanic activity or the collision of an object from space with Earth

endangered—in danger of disappearing forever

extinction—the state of being destroyed and gone forever

fertilizer—waste that adds nutrients and minerals into the earth

fossils—the old remains or evidence of plants and animals in rocks

grazing—eating grass and low-lying plants

hardpan—the ground that has been baked by the sun to be as hard as rock

Maasai—a group of African people living primarily in Tanzania and Kenya, known especially for their beautiful body decorations

migrations—the large movements of animals from one place to another, usually to follow their food sources

predators—animals that hunt and kill others for food

prey—an animal that is hunted and killed by another for food

prides—groups of lions that live, work, and play together

rhizomes—underground stems on grasses, similar to roots

safari—an adventure by people who go to explore an area for fun and education

saliva—the moisture created in the mouths of living things, used to help break down food when eating and digesting

social—forming cooperative relationships within a group

sward—a large expanse of grass

volcano—an opening at the surface of the Earth through which comes lava and gases

Index

About the Author

William Rice grew up in Pomona, California and graduated from Idaho State University with a degree in geology. He works at a California state agency that strives to protect the quality of surface and ground water resources. Protecting and preserving the environment is important to him. He is married with two children and lives in Southern California.